TO MAR:

WITH BEST WISHES

B. T. Serpell

BEN

— x —

TWIN BROOKS

WITH EXCERPTS FROM
SALTRAM: IN VISION & REFLECTION

&

SELECTED SATIRES

THE POEMS OF
BENJAMIN THOMAS SERPELL

A SECOND COLLECTION

First Edition
MMXVI

Darlington & Morley

First published in the United Kingdom in 2016 by
Darlington & Morley

ISBN 978-0-9956114-0-5

The right of Benjamin Thomas Serpell to be identified as the
author of this work has been asserted in accordance with the
Copyright, Designs and Patents Act 1988

Feature Characters by Jay Roerade

Other works:
WEST COUNTRY WAVES
SALTRAM: IN VISION & REFLECTION

www.benjaminthomasserpell.co.uk

CONTENTS

For my Madonna, my Sappho, and my beautiful Florentine;
for stirring my slumbers and waking my pen.

PREFACE

I

Three years have now passed since the publication of my first collection of poetry *West Country Waves*, and I find myself in the fortunate position of having garnered a small yet loyal readership; it is to them I owe this new collection. Where I once ambled blindly down that unknown path of publication, I now walk in the footsteps of experience. I have released my juvenilia, served my apprenticeship and learnt from my errors. Since then, I have stepped out in the company of my contemporaries, and schooled myself at their side. I have delved deep into the books of knowledge that adorn my walls, and sought that mystic character that lurks within us all, that true-self, that inner-voice. I have endeavoured to escape my high-glossed-fictions and to turn towards a poetry that carries at its core the romantic ideal; still I have dressed my poems in an elegance and form that is pleasing to both eye and ear, but I hope that under these loose-garments the principle of the poems remain and shine through. I leave it to the reviewers of today and the retrospective writers of tomorrow to judge.

My mind has a carelessness to wander, and my eye a foolish wish to rove; *Twin Brooks* is the result of this poor malady. I had the desire to charm my native surroundings into verse. Scattered among these pages there are to be found several glimpses of Plympton; from the church of St. Mary, to its neighbouring Priory; from the town's sylvan namesake the River Plym, to the twin brooks of our title, the Tory and the Longbrook; Plympton Castle and its Green are also versified in the Sapphonic Ode "The Valentine's Fayre". I owe a debt of gratitude to the late Joshua Brooking Rowe, whose writings on Plympton inspired a number of pieces.

There are compositions penned within the pleasant confines of my garden, and those scribbled loosely whilst sat upon a window's edge, those dreamt while in the fervour of stirred desire, and those mused over in the fresh life-affirming air of a scenic walk.

Reading over the poetic works I had gathered for inclusion I became aware of a sense of twinship flowing between the pieces, a sense that though each piece has a common origin they often ventured down different paths of experience. It can be said that two voices often guide our course, life decisions can be viewed as the splitting of a river; the calm course and the wild course. It is the romantic disposition to align oneself to the wild course, the torrent; that forged by Nature, unknown and unguided. Conservative man plots mindfully his course and favours the security of calmer waters, those whose flow has been governed and channelled, whose destination is set and expected.

The collection's sequence bears no relation to the order in which the works were written. My aim is to put out a coherent collection that can be read as a whole or in individual instalments. My arrangement of the sequence was governed by two main factors: the seasonal shift within the poems, and the emotional feelings which the works express.

Each poem has been written and formatted in a style which I hope is accessible to all. They are punctuated in what one might describe as general punctuation, allowing them to be read without unnecessary puzzlement, or indeed a need to hear them narrated by the author first. I am aware that in contemporary circles there has been a move to abandon the restraints of commas, colons, and full-stops etc. Although I note that these authors seem unable to distance themselves from the angelic charms of the flighty apostrophe; unlike many modern sign-writers. There also moves in our world a school of poetry that has abandoned the rules of capitalisation (in a punctuated sense), it can only be a short time before this school abandons both spelling and the formation of letters into words. I accept that my own compositions may contain words and language that some authors would deem antiquated and out-of-place in modern poetry. I would express that antiquated language is more commonly understood than a great deal of modern abbreviation and the closed school of academic terms, I'd further state that antiquated language is not to be confused with archaic language, which outside of a small and somewhat misguided authorship is quite lost to the modern world. Here I shall quote Wordsworth from his preface to the second edition of *Lyrical Ballads*: 'I have proposed to myself to intimate, and, as far as is possible, to adopt the very language of men...'

The Preface itself seems to have slipped from many a modern authors' mind, its ability to guide and ease the reader through an author's composition neglected. I have found as much joy in a well written Preface as I have in the body of work that follows one. The Preface is the poets' own prologue, his introduction and argument for that that follows. I confess to wondering if their absence from many modern compositions is not a sad reflection on our times, a reflection that many authors are simply writing for the sake of writing, and that the core of their poetry or prose is lacking an ideal, an essence of heart or argument. It may too be a reflection on the state of the publishing market, and the general materialism of modern society, an indelible mark upon our age. As Dante and Virgil climb, we seem to be forever descending into the abyss that they have fled. Could it be that man has grown content with Hell, and hungers only for the gold dust of Satan's purse, the adulterated images that stain his walls, and the lurid blasphemies of his wanton tongue. Here I fear we stray into argument, into the clouded haze of personal opinion, the blatant encroachment of the outside world and society onto the sensibilities of the individual; nay the Poet. Let me impose upon my reader the words of Romanticism's forgot trumpeter, that great Preface writer, journalist, essayist and author of *The Story of*

Rimini Leigh Hunt:

> A sensitiveness to the beauty of the external
> world, to the unsophisticated impulses of our
> nature, and above all, imagination, or the
> power to see, with verisimilitude, what
> others do not, —these are the properties of
> poetry;

So to place my argument in the purest of tongues and
most basic of languages: See; for that is what eyes are
for! Be not blind to the shackles of your freedom, the
chains of liberty, for the houses of oppression weigh
down upon us all.

II

To further expand on the concept of each work I have
taken the decision to offer a small explanatory
paragraph on a number of the pieces within the
collection.

"The Rime of a Country Wanderer" came about by a
play on the title of Samuel Taylor Coleridge's *The
Rime of an Ancient Mariner*. The piece was always
intended to be an opening, and it is my hope that it
sets the collection off with the message that is

repeated throughout, that that we are but a product of Nature and that our contentment is directly effected by the environment in which we place ourselves.

Later comes the work "White Violets", a lament, a realization that youth fades, and that flowers wilt; it also stands as a biographical record of what was and what has now become. A window looking back into the past of a faded childhood and out into an uncertain future.

"Encounters of Elegance" is one of many nods to the muses who have spun their enchantments over me during the writing of this collection. The work has a reference to Antonio Canova, the neoclassical sculptor of *Psyche Revived by Cupid's Kiss*. Encounters aims to show the spark and path of germination that occurs within any artist at that first point of inspiration; it is the old adage that beauty belongs to the beholder; if I were a diarist my journal would simple state 'today I met —' but mine is the malady to muse, the wish to capture a moment completely, to breathe into it more life than it could ever have held in its brief existence, to enchant it; as it enchanted me.

> It is the business of the Poet to communicate
> to others the pleasure and the enthusiasm
> arising out of those images and feelings in the
> vivid presence of which within his own
> mind consists at once his inspiration and
> reward
>
> – Percy Bysshe Shelley

"In The Chapel's Garden" is a work aimed at mirroring that of another author, in this case "She Dwelt Among The Untrodden Ways", one of the *Lucy Poems* by William Wordsworth. A poem that has always appealed to me greatly; in simple language we are drawn deeper and deeper into the unravelling heartbreak and despair of loss. "In The Chapel's Garden" is my own loose attempt upon this theme.

"In Fashion's Fairest Bloom" it was my wish to reassert that beauty is not as transient as society would like us to believe, the same theme is echoed in "To A Muse Bedecked In Diamonds". Both of these works carry at their heart the nakedness of beauty, that a dress or jewel, no matter how costly, is only an adornment upon the breathing soul that wears it. We must gaze past the trinkets and trappings of modernity to see the true beauty that bounds within us all. A sparkle of an eye can fuel a fancy, but it is the symphony of souls that captures the heart.

"Lines Composed in anticipation of a Promised Walk" contains a reference to Leigh Hunt's *The Story of Rimini*; my final lines are a reworking of the following quote taken from Hunt's third canto: 'The two divinest things this world has got, A lovely woman in a rural spot!' The work was originally planned for inclusion within my wandering poem *Saltram: In Vision & Reflection*, however due to its less factual and more dreamlike quality I chose to remove it. In truth the work bears no relation to Saltram at all, it is exactly as the rather clumsy title suggests, a poem of anticipation, a dream of a promised walk.

Throughout the collection there is a shifting of seasons. The works "Fair Nature's Play" and "A Moment" are probably the two that best display the waking of Spring. "Fair Nature's Play" being a work that simply describes the unfurling of a crocus; yet I have used the image of the waking crocus to mirror that joyous sense that those sensitive to nature experience at the shifting of Winter to Spring. "A Moment" also carries that essence of rebirth and release felt during those early days of Spring. The poem also contains a brief quote from the fourth line of Lord Byron's "She Walks In Beauty".

The triumphs of Spring are immediately followed by their sorrows. "Narcissus – A Lament" tells the story of the fading daffodil, confirming the mortality of nature; that there is lustre in youth, and if that lustre is not caught, dried and pressed, it will furrow and fade; such is the fate of the flower, and such is the fate of man.

"Rapture's Wicked Rush" sweeps us away from mortality and once more into the realm of realized beauty, unchecked desire, and aching's of the heart. The work carries echoes of Eve's seduction by the serpent within the garden of Eden. It again confirms the nakedness of beauty, and the grace of natural movement, a single line is quoted from Dante's *Divine Comedy:* 'There shines I know not what of the divine' This lines inclusion is designed to be both statement and question.

"Silhouette" continues the theme of realized beauty, and touches on the perils of desired perfection; it troubles me that so many walk this world unknowing of their own powers of inspiration. Those that have charmed my pen to verse have not fallen from the skies; those last four words are but the embellishments of fiction. We are all equally glorious in our deformity of unique creation; populate the world with stylized clones of theoretical beauty and you will breed the mundane, for fashions come and fashions go; it is the freak that always shines brightest amongst the crowd, the Pole Star of our dimmed galaxy.

"This England" is a work that should really have featured in my first collection *West Country Waves*, the fact that it wasn't written until after that book's publication is my only excuse. I have a rather unhealthy habit of penned odes to myself in which I'm curiously bobbing upon the sea. This work was no doubt written shortly after some unnecessary journey of great length, I am something of a gloomy traveller, highly aware of my own blessed surroundings, and with very little wish to part from them. This England is simply a romanticised account of one man's loathing of travel.

In "Ophelia Reborn" I have paired a personal encounter with that of the Shakespearean character immortalized in art. It was the painting by John William Waterhouse which I had most in mind when penning the poem. The opening is aimed at highlighting the doubts and unworthiness an artist can feel when confronted by a vision which has been replicated many times before.

"Dorian's Lament" was inspired by the well known fictional character Dorian Gray from Oscar Wilde's *A Portrait of Dorian Gray*. It is a poem written from his perspective and concerning the burdens of realised immortality. Might it not be argued that the intensity of pleasure is often heightened by its swiftness of existence?

"The Workshop" is a poem which was composed during my writing of *Saltram: In Vision & Reflection*, although not included in the final poem. A copy of Parmigianino's painting *Amor Carving His Bow* hangs within Saltram House, the poem expands upon Parmigianino's theme and places Amor in a woodland workshop.

The collection first ended with "What Am I Now?" a reflective poem on the passing of youth. I later decided on the inclusion of the two works "Stars of Hemlock" and "Promethean Rites", written as competition entries on the themes of Thomas Gray's *Elegy Written in a Country Churchyard*, and Mary Shelley's *Frankenstein; or, The Modern Prometheus* respectively.

Following the main collection are excerpts from the poem *Saltram: In Vision & Reflection* and pieces from a satirical collection about the first Laureate of Plymouth, I include individual Prefaces for these later in this volume.

III

As I look back over the works I have collected in *Twin Brooks* I am made aware of my evolution as a writer. My original idea was to have a collection solely focused on my home town of Plympton, only the strongest of these early pieces remain. The composition and completion of Book One of *Saltram* during the writing of this collection also withdrew some of the earlier material, and a certain amount of emphasis on locality. It is when I cast my reading eyes over *Saltram* that I become most aware of my growth as an author. The strength of that single composition to elevate and carry the reader to the poem's true ideal has not been lost on me, it has made me distinctly aware of how an epic poem often outweighs a collection of smaller pieces in emotive effect. The collection form does however offer a broader spectrum of subject matter and so appeals to a wider audience. I confess to catering to my already established audience, and to tastes which in my experience have proven to be profitable. As previously stated it is my hope that the romantic ideal burns through, but I am aware that I have included flippant works of fancy; which in truth I hope may act as a draw to readers yet to be stirred by higher poetics. Many of the poems began as a biographical record, simply romanticised and embellished in my hours of idleness for what one hopes is an appreciative audience. I dare say I will continue to mark the passing of time with many small biographical compositions, but it has now become my goal to turn towards a work of greater literary merit.

B. T. Serpell,
August 2016

TWIN BROOKS

The Rime of a Country Wanderer

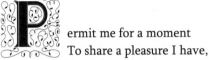

Permit me for a moment
    To share a pleasure I have,
To tell to all the joy I found
While wandering by myself.

The open world surrounds us,
So why imprisoned do we live?
Has mankind forgotten the joys
A pleasant walk can give?

To tread upon the earth,
To skirt the river's course,
To find our own fond path
That named The Great Outdoors.

To escape from our own comfort,
And be at the mercy of the skies,
To realise once more
What life is; naked of disguise.

To feel the breath of nature,
The heather at one's hand,
To gaze upon the waters,
And leave our footprints in the sand.

To be at last at liberty,
In actions and in mind,
To be once more with nature,
The womb of humankind.

The Music of St Mary's

olden hands on a clock's black face,
Count off with chimes: the noons, the days,
The months, the years of a Plympton man like I.
Peals of joy on a wedding day,
And a Tenor's toll;
That counts the memories of years away.
The music of St Mary's.

Eight bells toll - Eight bells ring;
To music's motion inverted they swing,
Handstroke and backstroke
Sally in hand then tail-end high,
The timbers creak the ropes they sigh,
Eight bells toll - Eight bells ring;
To the ears' of Plympton; blissful they sing,
From the granite tower to the priory's lawn,
Out over the thickets of holly and hawthorn,
To the swaying branches of oak and birch,
To the river's bend and the songbird's perch,
Eight bells toll - Eight bells ring;

Joy and love, and peace they bring;
To the Heavens above; in worship they sing.

White Violets

y wild flowers so dear,
Soon to be but memories;
Of my boyhood eye.
Forgotten like the hedgerows
And the verges,
Once tended by those who smiled
As I passed by.
Strangers are to come,
Change is in the air,
Forget me not my violets;
I was an infant to your care.
My periwinkles, my pimpernels;
Farewell, farewell,
Forget me not my wild bluebells,
Farewell, farewell.
Where once I wandered as a child,
I fear I shall not tread again,
My boyhood has now faded,
Must my England fade the same?

February Day

hat blue is this; that fills my Devon
sky?
What light is this; that shines this February
day?
Never before; their likeness have I seen,
Such gracious light, vivacious shades,
That fall and hang with wonder;
Above my own aged cot.
I have heard of their equal,
At Cornish coastal towns,
But not before this day,
Have they ventured Plympton's way.
Tis now four hours, since the bells of noon did
ring,
Twas three past the dawn, when first this scene
I saw,
The cloudless sky casts no shadows upon the
distant moor.
There is all the light of June,
Yet no warmth upon the breeze,
A Winter's chill still rides;

Begrudged upon the air,
The wind is heard,
But only in fleeting moments;
Is its movement seen,
Tickling snowdrops, charming laughter from
   the leaves;
Tis a most mysterious day,
I wait and watch,
For Spring to awake as the Autumn leaves
   decay.

Barren Beauty

leak and barren; describes my misty moor,
But there is beauty there, a beauty I adore,
Undressed among the elements:
The winds, the rain, the snow.
There lies beauty, with all her charms on show,
Her streamlets and her mires,
Her feather beds and gorse,
Her scattered stones and outcropped granite Tors,
Her barren beauty; hides no common flaws.

The mist descends upon her;
Catching strangers unaware,
Tis one of Nature's little jibes;
So always plan with care,
Go lightly on her pathways
And treat her beauty kind,
Or she'll draw you to her mires,
Where her feather beds you'll find,
For barren is her beauty; but deadly just the same,
Pay heed my dear rambler, for Dartmoor is her
name.

The Valentine's Fayre

Hear the laughs, tis Valentine's fayre,
To the green young loves, to the green
Maidens and masters dancing there,
Love's merry scene.

Purple twilight doth weave the sky
Amber flames lick Winter's air,
Love's own light in every eye
O joy is there.

To the green young loves, to the green,
Go win a kiss; Amour's embrace,
Lets passion's blushes mark your mien
As heartbeats race.

Hear the laughs, the joyful cheer,
Tis the merry din of revelry.
Affections fly to lovers near
Tokens penned so tenderly.

Becoming sights below the mount
Stir emotions and charm the eye,
More crimson cheeks that one could count
      Flush and flutter by.

Tis Valentine's fayre; love's own day,
Cupid's arrows are flying free,
Mirth and cheer in full display
      Such joy to see.

Encounters of Elegance

ncounters of elegance are the meetings
with my muse,
These are words that I have fashioned,
But I imagine they too are words that she might
choose;
For fashioned is she herself:
A Canova,
A sculpted grace,
Breathless Psyche in mortal form,
Dressed in the finery of creation's lucid eye
Those blooms of Eden,
That in rapture's moment the blessêd do espy.
Tis a death to meet her; a crossing of twin worlds,
From our Purgatory to the Paradise beyond;
There, there in those Elysium meadows my muse is
found:
Garlanded by the ivory orchids of eternal spring,
Serenaded by the Nightjars of Naxos,
And the lovesick ballads they do sing.
There where voiceless Echo wanders,
Mouthing, silent; these vapid words of mine.

In The Chapel's Garden

smoke trail is a-rising,
    Through the cloudless winter sky,
The frost is all but thawed now.
In the Chapel's garden,
Stands all that warms my eye.

A fire is gently crying,
A tender maiden; warming by its side,
Embers are a-glowing; crackling in the heat,
In the Chapel's garden,
Butterflies of ash; flutter to my maiden's feet.

O Joy, there are buds appearing,
Hyacinths bursting through the soil;
'Though their bells are yet to chime.
In the Chapel's garden,
One can reflect on all that's passed with time.

Beneath the rambling ivy,

Lies dear Lucy; *half hidden from the eye,*

A crown of moss; her velvet mane.

In the Chapel's garden,

Spring shall come; but my love shan't rise

again.

Words in italics taken from "She Dwelt Among The Untrodden Ways" by William Wordsworth.

Fashion's Fairest Bloom

Beauty hides not in nakedness alone,
   She whispers sweetly from your dress.
Her words are riddles of a radiance,
That your costume does confess.
From the cloud like satins
Loose upon your frame,
To the silks that sculpt you,
Plunging low at Cupid's claim.
Moon-white and panting,
Snowdrops with a pulse.
O the garments of our summer
Are like the petals of a rose.
Gentle and fragrant,
There to attract, there to adorn.
So breathe beauty to your garden,
Escape the mirrors of the dressing room,
Are you alone; not fashion's fairest bloom.

Plympton Priory

OPilgrim come, survey our scene,
A buried nave now turfed in green,
Quietening aisles lost to ripened time,
Little seems left of our Priory's prime.

But knowing eyes and knowing hands have
        tales to tell,
True there are those that know these ruined
        walls so well.
Beneath our feet — a wonder lost, the earth
        now holds,
With trowel and brush — a silent past unfolds.

So Pilgrim come and hear our tale,
That in days of yore to our Priory's port all
        ships did sail,
Twas from this cloister that Plympton grew,
In wealth, in riches; — and influence too.

But its noble grandeur gave way to woe,
When King and Pope came blow to blow.
The sacred stones were tumbled down,
And their wealth was robbed for a looting
crown.

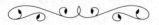

A Hundred Fragrant Bells

A hundred fragrant bells, hyacinths in
 bloom,
Pinks coyly blushing till the curfew of the
 moon.
Scented spring has awoken, breathed its
 perfume to the air,
Drawn me from my study to my garden's
 swinging chair,
Where the rambling clematis has taken
 flower,
Twined me with its runners, and held
 captive for this hour.
Songsters share their hymns, their pastoral
 elegies,
And I in Eden; pen tales I know with never
 please.

A hundred fragrant bells, golden trumpets
        on parade,
Am I honestly to believe that in chaos all
        was made?
That there is no formula for the beauty
        about my eye,
That careless chemicals miscollide as
        triumphed lovers sigh?
Petals gently peal, tulips bloom their soft
        skinned pastel shades,
Droplets of dew glisten and sparkle
        amongst the grassy glades.
Out of chaos, Chaos! All was born,
No wonder Godless man lives so bitter and
        forlorn.

To A Muse Bedecked In Diamonds

Are diamonds not but stones, when laid
upon a form so fair?
What sparkles do they harbour?
What brilliance could they bring?
To one so bathed, in flawless beauty's care;
What suitor could not the merest whisper
snare!

O Erato, let me ramble,
Let my wanton pen adorn,
Our Adonis; born of female form.

Tell now, what bring tiaras; to beauty's
templed crown?
For are those emblazoned eyes not stokers of
desire,
Do their lustrous cores not tantalize the soul?
Is that laid bare not the envy; of man, jewel
and gown?
Twin hazel oceans, in which, 'twould be pure
bliss to drown!

Death before beauty,
Rapture in a sigh.
Breathing as one, those tiny deaths we die.

Fair Nature's Play

O what is this? This beauteous
wonder I spy,
Peaking from the bed; before my musing
eye.
Violet is its colour, wineglass is its shape,
A charming little crocus; that this morning
did awake.

Awakened by the chorus; of the blue-tits
merry song,
Unfolding from its bud; as the welcome
sun gazed on.
A bloom; fragile in the breeze, yet
beautiful to view,
An infant of the soil; dabbed with morning
dew.

Why hath my eye here fallen? Upon fair
      Nature's play,
Have I unknown escaped; the burdens of
      my day?
For true, a joy is born; by this most natural
      sight,
A violet crocus; unfurled, casting shadows
      in the light.

Lines Composed in Anticipation of a Promised Walk

hough oft dim solitude has stung
my toiled brow,
I tie not this moment to those of yesterday.
For there dwells a pleasure in the waning of
the moon,
A promised encounter, that lights the vesture
of my discourse
And brightens my pen, to its blissful rills of
youth.

A leafy dream has awoken me to a joy as yet
unknown.
Lifted me from slumber, from those taunts of
mindless thought,
And carried me unknown; to this
resplendent dell.
Where the tuneful trickle of water has
stirred my sleeping ear,
And the heavy balm of perfumed Spring has
roused my senses more.

A shaded Eden, where golden beams of
        Easter light,
Break the leaf green dome above,
And sparkle white upon the rippling brook;
Their bended beams play gaily to my eye.
But my gaze is turned by a lilting call,
An offered hand, a glorious nymph sprung to
        life;
Standing, — beckoning.

Hand in fairest hand, to her pathless trail I
        turned,
Like twin doves her dancing feet skipped
        lightly on the ground,
Each bloom a little brighter as she passed,
For she brought and breathed sweet
        freshness to the air,
To her the pipers sung, the buds awoke,
And I dare say even silent Nature spoke,
Offered up some praise, breathed a gentle
        sigh,

Stole of her a stealth like kiss,
For each impression she left, a tiny step of
        bliss.
As we wandered on, I marvelled at my lot,
Nature's fairest daughter in love's divinest
        spot.

A Moment

Twas a warming April day,
That I and my companion wandered,
Conversing, with no chains upon our time.
When Nature spun a charm,
Silenced our lips — stole our gaze.
Proof no doubt that when idling
There are spirits that guide our ways.
Before us — the crown of Spring in bloom,
A thousand supernovas, bursting beauty, on
      each bending bough,
The majesty of Nature, at peace; charming
      every eye.
My companion took a picture,
Froze a moment to our day.
Now and evermore; *in her aspect and in her*
      eyes
I see those pink-white blossoms play.
And wonder;
What game Zephyrus eyed, when he blew
      this bliss my way?

Words in italics from "She Walks In Beauty" by Lord Byron.

Narcissus – A Lament

Wilting beauty bows before my eye,
No more do the golden flutes of
pleasure blow,
But tuneless trumpets sulk and sigh,
The dying daffodil; Narcissus has my eye.
His primrose petals withered,
Weighted down by woe,
His silken skin shuns its lustre,
Its youthful glow,
And I lament;
For in his image my fading muse I see,
Those passing graces that once triumphed
over me,
Now crisp and furrowed, that that was so
fair,
That that once shimmered and shone
before my glare,
O Narcissus, had I known; that death was
in my stare!

Fair Maid of May

air Maid of May, might I mirror
thee to my Devon sky?
For flawless is its beauty, and timeless its gaze
on me.
Tis on days as these, that Cupid's arrows are
said to fly;
And O how I wish those tiny darts would lay
their wounds in me.
Your tender eyes of fond affection, cloudless
their clarity,
Flutter them for but a moment, let me see
their beauties shine;
Playful are their charms, sparkling star-like
through my rhyme,
Should I take this to my heart, is this dear
Cupid's sign?
Fair Maid of May what other sight could man
compare to thee?
Surely from the Heavens thou has fallen this
auspicious day

For matchless are the Graces playing games
in front of me,
Breathing beauty's light, weaving loves
enchanted way.
Fair Maid of May! Beauteous as the warming
Devon sky
To thee I turn my eye, knowing again I reach
too high.

Rapture's Wicked Rush

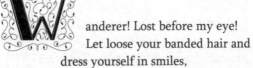anderer! Lost before my eye!
    Let loose your banded hair and
   dress yourself in smiles,
Let Zephyrs' perfumed breeze add fragrance to
      your blush,
Give-way; to the radiance of love,
And let your sighs join mine in rapture's
      wicked rush.

Sweet Eve! There are no apples here!
The tree hangs bare, for the knowledge has
      been shared,
Whispered to the orphans of the woodland,
To the stars of velvet night,
To our comely companions; of creativity's
      delight.

Pearls of decadence; ellipse the runway's aisle,
Bare but for the waves of creations gilded sea,
There shines I know not what of the divine.
But like Dantes' treasured line I wish it mine;
Raw and warmed by the heart that beats
       within.

Wanderer! Stalking to the camera's beat!
Strike no pose for warmer be by-far the beauty
       of movement's grace,
Far-off and vacant are the stares of vogue's
       decorum.
Yet lift not your eyes to mine,
For my heart's own pulse intends to lead you
       out of time.

Sweet Eve! I know your weakness!
The rush you long to feel, the fruit you yearn
    to taste,
The powdered leaves of pleasures high, the
    juices of the vine.
For I am cursed the same!
Poisoned by the ivy that wreathes this crown
    of mine.

Pearls of decadence; skim sweet nectar's
    stream,
Dazzling the eyes of all caught upon the scene,
Mirroring the sparkle that shines above your
    pleasured smile.
Your fragrant blush has peaked, travelled
    upon your skin,
Warmed and joyed by the lusts that pulse
    within.

Wanderer! Gazing from the edge;
Lend not your ear to me.

Words in italics from *The Divine Comedy* by Dante Alighieri

Turning Sappho

reamer I, dreamer I,
Had I but wings to fly,
They'd beat and beat,
Till broken gravity,
Lay in defeat.

Then upward I'd climb,
So high would I soar,
I'd curve my course,
To Mytilene's shore,
Where I would rap,
Fair Sappho's door.

But oh!
How I sigh,
For what chance have I,
To woo the loving,
Lesbian's eye.

Dreamer I, dreamer I.

Silhouette

Silhouette, shadow of light,
Fair beauty behind a screen,
Grace in contours, delicately drawn,
By the Artist of our fates.

A candle flickers at your side,
It warms a pulse, a pulse so slow but sure,
There's a warmer life within you,
A truth to which your eyes must turn.
For creation's gift shines not in mirrors,
Nor images of false reproach.
But Art's own eyes do spy it,
And sculpt its living air.

Strain not your eyes on fate's horizon,
That distant, distorted haze,
Tis a false mirage you see.

Flicker, flutter, goes life's limpid flame;
O child could I in my meekness place a value
        to your name?
For silhouettes are fine, fine and well for
        picture walls,
But silhouettes offer but a glimpse, a glance;
Of that that's beating there within.
For there is beauty in emotion,
As there is beauty in each breath,
So breathe my dear child;
Leave us not bereft.

To an Enchantress Informed of Her Charms

arewell, farewell fair mystery of mine,
I'll wear no shrouds in living time,
But give my soul to sprites of rhyme,
To tidings and tales of moments true,
For what good is falsehood when love's in
       view.
True reckless I shall bare my all anew!
Doubt no longer; Enchantress awaken,
Could such a hand truly rest untaken?
Hark! Hark now the songsters waken,
Piping poesies gay and hymns divine,
Could I but mingle their strains with mine,
Then I would charm such words to rhyme,
That reading eyes would learn to waltz,
And steady hearts would tremble weak,
            at every pulse.

This England

Beckon me not to dull and distant lands,
To far-famed Cities that for lost reasons I
should know.
No leave me to the sea,
To the free will of the waves,
They'll wash me to my own dear native
shore,
And there! With hands a-clasp of sand,
My lion heart shall roar,
O tis England, this England I adore.

I fair Albion's son need no knowledge of the
Nile,
The Amazon of my eye,
Is my own dear native Plym alone.
Flowing softly to the Sound,
Falling freshly from the moor,
Upon the wavelets of her breast,
My heart it beats, my soul doth soar,
Tis England, this England that I adore.

So breathe not the breath of far-off desert
       climes,
Into these Devonian lungs of mine,
Sweet and scented is the air that dwells
       within,
Charmed by the blossom upon the breeze.
No I need not venture far, refrain, do not
       implore,
Breathless would thou be;
If thou could see the nature at my door,
For tis England, fair England I adore.

The Sound is a bay on the English Channel at Plymouth

Could Flowers Be The Answer?

ould flowers be the answer?
Could a bouquet fair and fragrant,
Scent and colour the verse
That I so long to pen?
Could a clutch of Nature's blooms
Rouse that smile of joy again?
Bring a crimson blush of colour,
To beauty's lovelorn cheek?
Could I have found the answer
For when a poet's pen falls weak?
Is not the truest verse of all
That, that Nature's tongue does speak?

I picture them being passed,
Into her gentle welcome hands,
With sparkles of surprise
Her youthful eyes aglow.
Unfolding the gifter's note
With a rush and wish to know,
Is it he? Is it he?
Come, come fair maid;

What other man of England,
Would send flowers to the sea!

Ophelia Reborn

What line could breathe to life; those
    virtues I have seen?
What foolish thought, hath entered this
    musing mind of mine?
That I; I myself alone could find strength of
    words to tell?
That I could cast once more that famed
    enchanted spell,
That I could paint that picture, that doth so
    hold the artist's eye,
That I could place before thee, that that only
    darkness could deny?
True I mask not my doubts, I own them now
    to you.
Yet proceed I must, in vain belief
That of Ophelia's grace my lines shall find a
    fitting truth to tell.

Unknown was it to I; that on that day we'd
        meet,
That in that drape hung corner, such an image
        I would greet.
Ophelia! Arisen! Roused and awakened from
        the waters golden bed,
An image on which all arts faithful eyes have
        hungered and have fed.
Fair Ophelia, sweet rose of May,
There before me with her enchanted tresses of
        glowing amber flame.
O let not my feeble words dishonour the
        passions that mark her name.
What warmth it was that radiated from that
        enlightened soul,
Those fiery glances that did not burn,
But surely temper the steels that shape my
        very whole.
Aflame was that moment, aflame its memory
        still;
A flame that did not Man nor Nature ill.

Burn enlightened spirit, burn!
Where and to what could these my captivated
eyes now turn?
Turn from her, her who holds such sensual
charms,
With glowing embers, fiery thoughts and
kohl-less smoking eyes.
I breathe, I breathe these honest words,
As again, again with memory's flash
Her whitened breast does sink to rise,
Her panting bosom where fortunes favourite
the opius lotus lies.
Fair Ophelia, amber flame, I but pen to praise
The mirrored glowing of the Sun's own rays.
Crowned are they by garlands, those sweet
blooms of Nature's grace,
How worthy they of their beaming dwelling
place.
Burning heart, enlightened mind,
Onward; onward through creations world
your course must wind.

Tender eve, gentle night,
Weave no mysteries of how Art's fire does find
    its light.
For alight it is; and by her own flame,
O fair Ophelia, wear proudly this; Art's gifted
    name.

The character of Ophelia comes from the play *Hamlet* by William Shakespeare, this work was inspired by the painting *Ophelia* 1894 by John William Waterhouse.

A Truth

resh the breeze that lifts
fragrance to the air.
Among the lavender fields I wander.
A carpet of mauve colouring the hillside;
Awaiting the reaper's blade.

Approaching, I spy a stranger.
A fellow wanderer,
Lost to the solitude of thought.

Our paths meet.
Tis a woman; she starts,
And whispers without words
A truth our lips could never speak.

The Edge

'T was an unbecoming day,
No warning siren sounded,
No declaration was declared,
But moment led to moment;
As night-time; charmed reserve away.

Aimlessly; we wandered,
Down those cobbled pathways,
Passed the factory's wharf,
The sleeping citadel,
With Hardy's girl behind;
Blithe as blithe could be.

Was that our weakness?
The indifference that we shared,
Two tarnished hearts, paired as one,
The night our own; silent and still.
Phantoms dressed in shadows.

Words in italics taken from "The West of Wessex Girl" by Thomas Hardy.

Italian Aromas

The hour of slumber beckons,
The sable spirits of night,
Have drawn the curtains upon my day.
I've retired to my chamber,
Scribbled my thoughts,
Downed my pen, quaffed my tonic and
snuffed the flame.
All is dark, all is still;
To the realm of sleep I gift my will.

A fragrant breath breathes beauties to my night,
A kiss from the pillow where late my love did
lie,
Breathing heavy breaths of pleasure, and
triumph's golden sigh.
But absent, absent now is she, absent as the
candle's faded light;
No more kisses shall I spill upon her throat so
white.

That Tuscan meadow where all of Eden's bliss
      did lie,
Caressed by raven locks, that in both beauty
      and air did vie.
Breaths of Florence, Italian aromas, rue and
      mourn her distant flight,
As I alone; toss and turn in this flower bed of
      mine.
A scented pillow, a burnished rose, now all
      that's left
Of a loose love whose lingering breath has me
      bereft.
Was she a passing spectre, a vision, or
      something more divine?
For though I now lay absent, of her amorous
      company,
Each breath I breathe brings back her scented
      kiss to me.

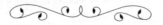

Dorian's Lament

reathe not your dreams into the
madness that is me,
True time I have halted, but tis not the past
but the present I flee.
Well I know what I know, tis the unknown
wonders that I so fear,
Those secret mysteries that with each
careless stroke,
My Wilde pen draws near.

Evermore; innocent eyes appear,
Naked; luminous, bewitching.
At the silver mirror I stand and wonder,
What have I become, where has my riddle
run?
Poison on my lips, a temptress at my ear,
A dozen tiny deaths draw near
Are we ever, what we appear?

No stains now show, upon my pure white
            soul;
Unblemished I!
But I've tainted tears within my dry blue
            eyes,
A smoke screen,
That hides the honesty; of all my lies?

A painted portrait is all I am,
A frozen moment from another time.
A flower whose fragrance never fades,
Plucked from the spring fed Elysium glades.
Beauty my burden, charm my shackled
            chain,
To love me; is a transient bliss on the path to
            pain,
To love me, is to love in vain.

Inspired by Oscar Wilde's novel *The Picture of Dorian Grey*

The Madonna in Tears

I saw the virgin mother weep
Saltless tears of innocence undone,
Her ivory pallor bejewelled,
And though she spoke no words,
Well I read the sorrow; that seized her
tongue.

Upon her cheeks, crystal streams of sadness
ran,
Remorseful, I dwelt on the consciousness of
man.
That beauty belongs to the beholder,
That malady mars us all,
That eyes will ever wander,
And that man will ever fall.
For temptation is not attained,
But merely breaking from within.
Mortal man; predisposed to sin.

Thus I ponder;
Am I searching for a saviour?
Am I awaiting a calling?
Am I in the innocence of life,
Unconscious that I'm falling?

Woken by woe, silenced by image,
Roses breathe, tears run,
And I am moved;
O I am done.

Meanderer of the Midnight Hour

 eanderer of the midnight hour;
Might I wander a while, restless at
your side?
For though day's toil has left me weary,
Absent lies my pillow of yawning sleep.
So I dear Tory join you,
On the path your waters gently creep.

Moonlit companion; lull my misty mind,
Take my troubles upon your current,
Ferry them — far from where I now stand.
Meander, beneath the timid bliss of moon,
Shine on in peaceful splendour;
And sleep shall find me soon.

The Tory is a brook and tributary to the river Plym

The Workshop of Love

Shavings fall, tapers fly; ringlets of desire.
Amor is carving his tender shafts of love,
Smooth and streamline, each a whittled dove.
Close by sits Erato plucking melodies from
    her lyre;
Sparks of passions flare from off their
    woodland fire.
Honey vapours plume, ethereal spirits of love,
Escaping our world for the higher one above.
Sweet aromas of arousal, delicate draughts of
    desire
Breathe into the Dryads' fragrant grove.
Amor crafts on, his darts now winged and
    tipped.
Nymphs dance giddy on the incense they
    have sipped.
Yawning Eve awakens, dons her dress of
    mauve.
For the arts of love Amor is now equipt,
With bow, full quiver; and love's romantic
    script.

Winter's Kiss

ark December's dawned,
Winter's Nymph has awoken,
And I; passion's fool,
Have charmed her well.
Her glacial eyes, her blue-veined soul,
Her snow white breasts, shimmering,
shivering,
Sultry as a solstice yet to dawn;
Far from the flames of *Mordor* was her white
spirit born,

To the night our own, my silver pen shall turn,
Wilful she stumbled to the shelter of my home.
To the decadent comfort of my low lit
chamber,
Where she warmed me not with words,
But touched me with her chill,
Kissed and breathed, her breathless cold to me.
Wrapped me; in the sorcery of her fever.

Now whitened by her love,
I lay my weary limbs to rest.
My midnight Merlot has been supplanted,
No shapely glass of sweet intoxication,
Do I have strength to hold.
A burning mug of deeper hue,
Now warms these shaking hands of mine.
If only, its clouding vapours could burn her
        kiss away.

But Winter's Nymph is stubborn, spiteful.
She clings feverishly to me;
O were she but as loose and as free,
As her sisters of summer,
Who spill their kisses just for fun,
Then her whitened frame would have left me
        long ago.
But No! She clings, like the morning frost,
The unthawed snow, the creaking ice of a
        death-trap lake,
And I; passion's fool, know well the bliss of my
        mistake.

The word *Mordor* is taken from *The Lord of the Rings* by
J.R.R. Tolkien, however my reference originates in the song
Ramble On by Led Zeppelin.

A Ring Without Words

ring without words speaks not the
    tongue of love,
Tis but a silver band:
A void,
An emptiness.
Gifted with what?
A wish?
A want?
A desire that one dares not speak?

Is this the climax; of love's romantic peak?
No, no my dove — gracious are the words of
    love;
Gifted without want or weight,
Like butterflies of bliss;
Adornments to each kiss.

Twin Brooks

y love and I wander; in December's winter chill,
Hand in hand with equal pace we stroll,
To the twin brooks of Plympton.
The Tory; swollen, brown and raging.
The Longbrook; silent, still and clear.

Mirrors to our souls I wonder?
Parallel brooks;
Twin courses;
Tributaries — running into one.

Both the Tory and Longbrook are tributaries to the river Plym

To A Tear, Loose Upon A Loved One's Cheek

ere my tongue as measured as my pen,
A sweeter song I'd sing,
Not tears but smiles my lustrous words would
bring.
I'd take my time, tell it true,
Toss my scribbles of rashness to the floor,
Open up and let my innermost feelings pour.
O were I free from the madness of man's own
poison,
I'd not fret about the future, the unmapped
road ahead,
No; I'd dwell with a passion though; on those
three words she said.
I'd play that scene over, over and over
through my cluttered mind,
Recalling her frankness, her fervour,
Her weighted silence through which she
wished my troubled heart to speak;
That lost moment, when a loose tear
moistened my loved one's cheek.

Were I but the mirage she dreams, that walks
among these mortal men,
I'd score through that moment gift my tongue
the passions of my pen,
Dry her tears, and weep my own.

The Snub

 marked your exit, your hasty flight,
The snub that set my mind amusing,
That melancholy night.

Did you spy my amorous eyes awander?
As they crossed the room,
And fell in daze upon her.

Did you hear my little heart aflutter?
As she raised a bashful smile,
And blushed, at the comment her friend did
utter.

Tell me my lady, tell me true?
Is my pen of poesy now bound to you,
Can I not turn its playful tip
To the attractions of another?
For though the odds seem high,
Not every muse; becomes my lover.

What Am I Now?

hat am I now? Now that the haze
of youth has gone,
And the ghosts of my revelries return.
Dressed in their drunken guises,
Wrapped in the stained silks and satins of our
decanted decadence,
And loud, loud with their wild and wagging
tongues of torment.
Humming loose their vapid hymns of spent
amour.

O the scorching eyes of scolded youth, how
they burn!
Midnight is mine no more.

Fair Sleep embrace me, cloud my cluttered
         mind,
For restless here I lie, counting back my
         misspent days,
My tangled tales of toxic passions-impure.
Soothe my fever, quell my heart and ferry me
         off to Hades shore.
For all is not forgotten, though liberty is lost to
         me.
Wayward must I wander? Downward must I
         fall?

Those painted nails still scour my soul,
And sure am I those burgundy lips taste me
         even now.

The two following pieces were written specifically for the Thomas Gray Anniversary Competition 2016, and The Keats-Shelley Prize 2016. They are based on the respective prompts of 'Full many a flower was born to blush unseen' from Gray's *Elegy Written in a Country Churchyard*, and the theme of *Frankenstein; or The Modern Prometheus* by Mary Shelley.

Stars of Hemlock

teal me away from the sorrowed sighs of suburban nature's weeping eye. Take me from the ordered beds and structured margins of restrained advance. Those hanging cages where that once wild is tamed, manicured; manipulated; set and formed to the docile doctrine of man's material dream. O let me loose in the wilderness of disorder's rambling confusion. Let me lie amongst those hidden groves, those secret bowers where the mutinous blooms of nature blush unseen. Steal me from the neon watch-lights of our nocturnal day, and let me rest! Lost beneath the cloudless sky of contemplation, the great white stars of the hemlock flower. Lulled and at peace where the solemn yews and moonlit stones in silence stand. Pass me back to nature, back to the chaos of my birth.

Promethean Rites

The cryptic code of Chaos is dripping from beyond.

Another thousand martyrs stand ready for the cause.

We've formulas and fables, breakthroughs gifting hope,

Unravelling Chaos's riddle into a language all can read,

Breaking into atoms and elements every segment of the seed.

Plucking ribs from the dying and moulding them in clay,

Chasing down the catastrophe of creation, the primal spark

That lit the fire from which Prometheus stole the flame.

That flame that now burns white below our furnace.

Ancient ores liquefy, their vapour's breathe
　　　secrets to the air,
Captured and distilled; into the elixir of our
　　　dreams.
A tonic to the path of knowledge, to unify
　　　creation and creator.
Elucidating the mysteries; once shrouded in
　　　Abyss.

SALTRAM: IN VISION & REFLECTION

INTRODUCTION

The following three pieces are excerpts taken from my narrative poem *Saltram: In Vision & Reflection*. I have included them in this volume to allow a wider audience to encounter a work that only had a limited run as a bespoke artisan pamphlet. The excerpts are taken from Book One, the project is as yet unfinished. The full poem is told as a narrated walk through the grounds of the Saltram estate. The following is taken from the Preface of *Saltram: In Vision & Reflection*:

> The Estate of Saltram sits on the southern banks of the River Plym in Devonshire, it is a short distance from the coastal city of Plymouth. Closer still, is the Stannary town of my own residence, Plympton. The Saltram Estate comprises of a Georgian Mansion surrounded by beautiful gardens and landscaped parkland, within which there is to be found a Stable block, Orangery, Chapel, and several follies. The Estate has been in the possession of The National Trust since the 1950's, prior to which it was the private residence of the Parker family (the Earls of Morley).

A Childhood Reflection

irst to meet my eye is the light of morn;
Bright and young, sparkling where the
dabbled ducks
Do glide, breaking the stilled surface, to a
Thousand ripples, uniformed but rare; tilted
Mirrors reflecting the sun's white glare. I
See my childhood image; mirrored, a portrait
Writ in water, timeless as a phrase.
Over the painted fence I lean, as a
Child beneath its rail I'd peep, slipping
My hands between the spindles, reaching to
All beyond, those wonders of the deep. My
Memories now live, through the child at
My feet, fresh to the world, awake to Nature's
Spell; a betokened youth on whom my shadow
Fell.

Away, away I turn; with fertile
Memories blossoming bright, shooting colours
Through my blissful mind, taking me from this
Moment to those of yesteryear, those drifted
Days and hours of youthful flight, when all

Bloomed fresh before my eye, all innocent
In discovery, free from *learned subjection*,
Wanton glances and envies bitter bite.

The words in italics are taken from the self-penned epitaph of
John Keats.

Fanny's Bower – The Temple of Jupiter

There is an orchestra, masked among the
Shrubbery; tuneful and melodious,
For joy alone they play. Lost to literature;
They are the ambience of my day. At
Turn of page, I lift my eye, to merry
Songsters scavenging loose upon the thicket's
Floor, where twig and leaf lie fallen, Nature's
Carpet; golden-crisp and brown. Upward rise
Twin columns, Tuscan in their form, granite
Props smoothed and shaped by the knowing hands
of

Man. Fanny's Bower – sanctuary, amount
The vale, Temple of Jupiter, bathed in
Pastoral hymn. Yet there is a sadness
Here; that shrouds my native Plym.

A Flutter of Butterflies

Willowherb to
Lavender, lavender to willowherb.
I spy the playful butterflies, dancing
Their amours. Demurely dressed in dusty
Browns, waltzing weightless through perfumed
air, to
The honeysuckle high, then sweeping low,
To geraniums below. From flower
To flower, petal to leaf, leaf to petal
Onward through my scented bower, where the
Clematis twines its chosen course. A flutter
Of butterflies; dancing like the Hours,
Upon the morning air. Black veins, lace their
Velvet wings, where opulent eyes of golden
Orange burn, weightless, and wondrous.

SELECTED SATIRES

PREFACE

Disillusionment is such a fine frailty when its victim hopes only for escape, when one has the carelessness to crave exposure and the vanity for praise it becomes nothing more than a shackle of lunacy. Sadly, such was the case with the first Laureate of Plymouth. The following poems were written during the gloomy days of his administration, an administration marked out by the bleakness and contempt that leached from the weekly offerings of Plymouth Poet Laureate Mike Sullivan.

This collection is not the place to fully expand my views on the questionable appointment of Plymouth's first Poet Laureate, our current Laureate Emeritus. Indulgence is a vanity I save for more pleasurable scribblings. It is worth noting however that on completion of the Laureate's first year of office (October 2014) I published the satirical pamphlet *Lessons For Larry*, this included a lengthy Preface along with breakdowns (lessons) of five satires and their inspirations. From that collection only our opening piece "Versifying Vomit" is included, the second and third pieces were composed during the second year of administration.

The full number of works composed upon the theme of laureate-mocking escapes me. I had intended to include the work "The Necessity of Knowledge" which questioned the process that led to the election of Plymouth's first Poet Laureate, but as there now appears to be a more open and accountable process of election the inclusion of this work would gain little. It saddens me that my readers will not have the pleasure of enjoying "The Dunce in the Dolphin" in full, a work inspired by Mr Sullivan's "The Dolphin", and the work which led to the christening of The Dolphin School; maybe one day I'll write a volume on my dear Dolphins, our canting contemporaries, to whom this section of my collection is dedicated.

> The Dolphin's fire all roaring flame,
> Burning sparks into the room it spits,
> Where scribbling fast the bard he sits,
> Our noble dunce; the muse of wits.

From "The Dunce in the Dolphin"

Versifying Vomit

A satire on the work "Bring Us Your Sick"
by Michael Sullivan, Laureate of Plymouth

y dear laureate of frail verse and
humorous request,
On the subject of satire it's said that Dryden's
pen was best,
And though I'm no physician I've a mind to
raise the dead,
See I find myself in a humour after reading that
that I have read.
Of all the titles that mortal man could conjure
"Bring us your sick",
Surely tis a jest, a red rag to our wit?
Who would beckon nausea, when one could
have applause from the pit?
Is our playhouse thus to be plagued by those in
poets' masquerade,
Might there not be scribblers and satirists
lurking coyly in the shade.
With steady minds, ready pens, sharp and eager
wit;

Poised to stir convulsions of laughter, rather
        than the bile some emit.

For true there is a Distance, between your verse
        and mine,

Mine is dressed in flounces, with gay charms to
        every line,

While yours is much more weighty and rather
        sluggish to digest,

Thus indeed there is some sense to the retchings
        you request.

To purge one's self abruptly, is an action I
        commend,

For minds are fragile fellows, and once
        corrupted, seldom mend.

So friends! Be wary of what you read, mindful
        of all you see,

Guard yourselves well from purveyors of
        notoriety.

Tread light on poesy's path, chase not merits nor
        marks of glory,

Find that inner voice, and you'll find a brighter
        glory.

And there, there in short; is the moral of our
        story.

But back to wit and whim,
And the regurgitated metaphors in which
       together we now swim.
Head, head up high my laureate! Don't let the
       critics drag you down.
The rank and rancid gutter is no place for
       poesy's laurelled crown.
Saunter through the sick-house, 'orderly of
       rhyme',
Salute the surgeons, the nurses,
Maybe see a doctor about the weakness of your
       verses.
They have length, but will they have longevity,
       in their absence of direction?
At commencement did I not promise Dryden's
       resurrection,
I quote:

> though Heaven made him poor, with reverence
>   speaking,
> He never was a poet of God's making;
> The midwife laid her hand on his thick skull,
> With this prophetic blessing – Be thou dull;
> Drink, swear, and roar, forbear no lewd delight
> Fit for thy bulk, do anything but write.

Eat opium, mingle arsenic in thy drink,
Still though mayest live, avoiding pen and ink.
I see, I see, tis council given in vain,

Know: I need no titles of fancy to dignify my
name.

The words quoted are taken from *Absalom and Achitophel*
by John Dryden.

On The Death of a Poem

A satire on "The Death of a Poem"
by Michael Sullivan, Laureate of Plymouth

eep and low the sombre bell of grief
does toll.
From the hearse the sable casket, raised and
drawn,
The grieving crowd hang their heads and mourn;
Death has dawned. Dead the poem of callow soul,
Lit for a moment — a flash, a spark upon the coal.
But though that flame did flicker; no life did wake,
Smothered at birth! For the good of all Art's sake.
Spat forth by he who bemoans the laurelled role,
Crippled by critique; foul cries our wounded fool.
So sure that praise is what the world does owe
him,
Could he but stop and think; who killed his poem?
Was it Southey, Pye or The Cockney School,
Gifford's Quarterly or Murray's Edinburgh
Review?
No! Mike Sullivan, Laureate Emeritus; the killer
was you.

The Good Ship Laureate

O Larry! Dear Larry! So the maiden
voyage is done,
The good ship Laureate beached! Aground she's
safely run,
Both mutiny and desertion have left not a
living soul aboard.
A stormy course of wayward verse that only
Dolphins dare applaud,
That rowdy school of half-cut bards,
Who drink to write,
And write to drink,
But never stop to think!

Sense and dignity circle; the albatross and
raven,
Shrieking down at the Laureate, upon her
sandy haven.
There's a party at her keel waiting for the tide
to send her back adrift,
For the Laureate's shadow is something of a
satire! In the style of Swift!

Tudor's *Titanic*, Sullivan's *Bounty*,
A Dolphin out of water,
A drunk without a drink,
A vessel doomed to sink.

O Larry! Dear Larry! I hear you're in the gin,
Keep up your spirits! Take it on the chin!
Remember the banquet, you're place of honour,
      captain of the table.
Now deserted the good ship Laureate awaits a
      captain more able!
They're offering all the gin in Plymouth,
For a Drake, a Scott,
A native son or daughter;
Well versed; in bailing water!

Larry a local nickname for The Plymouth Poet Laureate. The
name Tudor refers to Tudor Evans leader of Plymouth City
Council at the time the Laureate roll was created. Both the
Titanic and *HMS Bounty* are ships with unfortunate histories.

Index of first lines

Index of first lines

Acknowledgements

My thanks and gratitude go to all who have read this volume. I thank William Telford and Kenny Knight for a friendship that has grown side-by-side with the literature ambitions that fill this collection. I extend my thanks to Steve Spence and Sara Elizabeth Smiles for proofreading the manuscript, all errors remain my own. My thanks to The Athenaeum Writers' for their honest critique on the works that came to fill this collection. I thank Jay Roerade for the feature-characters and scroll designs that feature within. Furthermore I wish to thank the independent retailers who have been kind enough to stock my works, especially Jack and Maggie. The literature clubs and organisations who have invited me to feature, The Language Club, CrossCountry Writers and The Word. My thanks to The Saturday Poem and Literary City of The Plymouth Herald for publishing my works, and their continued support of literature in Plymouth.

Darlington & Morley